EMERGENCY!

PLANE CRASH

Nicola Barber

Arcturus

This edition first published in 2011 by Arcturus Publishing

Distributed by Black Rabbit Books
P.O. Box 3263
Mankato
Minnesota MN 56002

Printed in China

Library of Congress Cataloging-in-Publication Data

Barber, Nicola.
  Air crash / Nicola Barber.
    p. cm. -- (Emergency!)
  Includes bibliographical references and index.
  ISBN 978-1-84837-956-5 (lib. bdg. : alk. paper)
  1. Aircraft accidents--Juvenile literature. I. Title.
  TL553.5.B285 2012
  363.12'4--dc22

2011006630

Series concept: Alex Woolf
Editor and picture researcher: Alex Woolf
Designer: Ian Winton

Picture credits
Anynobody: 14.
Chensiyuan: 10.
Corbis: cover (HO/Reuters), 4 (Bettmann), 6 (Kyodo/Reuters), 7 (Vince Streano), 9 (Bettmann), 11 (Dexter Alley), 15
(Tony Comiti), 17 (Santiago Ferrero/X02264/Reuters), 20 (Bettmann), 21 (Bettmann), 22 (Sean Adair/Reuters), 23
(Neville Elder), 24 (Larry Downing/Reuters), 25 (Lucas Jackson/Reuters), 27 (EFE TV/epa).
fr.academic.ru/dic.nsf/frwiki/33909: 26.
Getty: 12 (Popperfoto), 13 (Keystone/Hulton Archive), 16 (Julian Wasser/Time & Life Pictures).
Rex: 29 (Eric C Pendzich).
Shutterstock: 5 (Semenova Ekaterina), 8 (Songquan Deng), 28 (Xavier Marchant).
www.digitalgothic.net: 19.

Cover picture: Rescue workers spray water into the wreckage of a plane that crashed at Yogyakarta Airport,
Indonesia, in March 2007. Twenty-one passengers and one crew member died in the crash.

Every attempt has been made to clear copyright. Should there be any inadvertent omission, please apply to the
publisher for rectification.

Supplier 03, Date 0411, Print Run 1051
SL001698US

Contents

The First Crash

In September 17, 1908, an excited crowd of around 2,000 people gathered at Fort Myer, Virginia. They had come to see the flight of the Wright *Flyer*, a plane designed by brothers Wilbur and Orville Wright. Only five years earlier, the Wrights had made the first successful powered flight in history. Now, Orville Wright was about to demonstrate the latest version of the *Flyer*, built for the US army.

Propellor failure

The army wanted a plane that could carry passengers. After two successful flights with a passenger on board, on September 17 it was the turn of Lieutenant Thomas E. Selfridge to go up into the air. With Orville Wright at the controls, the *Flyer* completed several circuits about 150 feet (45 m) up in the air. Then Orville heard several taps and two big thumps—a propeller had broken.

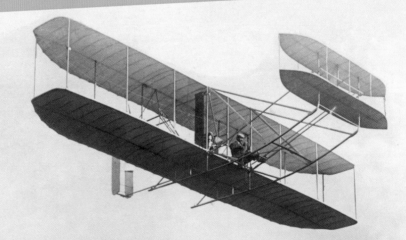

Orville Wright at the controls of the Wright *Flyer* at Fort Myer on September 9, 1908, eight days before the crash that killed Thomas E. Selfridge.

The first fatality

The *Flyer* went out of control and nosedived into the ground. Both pilot and passenger were thrown against the plane's wooden framework. Orville Wright was badly injured, but Selfridge fractured his skull and died later that day. Sadly for him, Selfridge became the first person to be killed in an air crash.

Modern planes such as this Boeing 737 carry millions of people safely around the world every year.

SAFETY IN THE SKIES

Air travel has developed very quickly since those early days. Today millions of people take to the skies every year, and air travel is extremely safe. But unlike the Wright brothers' *Flyer*, modern planes are huge. When air crashes do happen, they often kill hundreds of people.

After a Crash

All airports have their own fire services, ready to deal with any emergency. If a plane has a problem during takeoff or landing, help is at hand very quickly. Airport fire crews practice their drills over and over again so that they are ready for an emergency at any time of day or night.

Rapid response

Speed is vital, because fire can spread quickly through a plane. With their fast, powerful trucks, firefighters can be pumping foam onto an aircraft fire within two minutes of an emergency call. If the firefighters can control the fire, the passengers inside have a better chance of escaping.

Airport firefighters put out a fire on a crashed cargo plane at Narita International Airport in Chiba, Japan.

SAVING LIVES

Manchester Airport, England, August 22, 1985: One of the engines of a British Airtours plane caught fire as the aircraft began its takeoff. Despite a rapid response from the airport fire services, the fire spread through the plane. Choked by thick, black smoke and flames, 55 people died in the blaze. After this tragedy, safety was improved in all planes to give people more time, and chance, of escaping a fire.

Investigation

Once a rescue is over, it is important to try to find out why the accident happened. The wreckage is left in place for accident investigators to examine and photograph. It is their job to work out what went wrong—and how similar accidents can be avoided in the future.

Of course, not all aircraft crashes happen in airports. In this book you can find out about all sorts of accidents, and how the emergency services dealt with them.

Accident investigators examine the remains of a jet engine after a collision between an airliner and a small private plane in California.

Empire State Building, 1945

It was a foggy morning in New York City, July 28, 1945. Lieutenant-Colonel William Smith was at the controls of a US army B-25 bomber, on his way to pick up his commanding officer. But as he flew, Smith picked up an ominous warning from air traffic control at New York Municipal Airport: "We're unable to see the top of the Empire State Building. Suggest you land here."

Lost in the fog

Smith ignored the suggestion that he should land. Surrounded by thick fog, he lost height in the hope of seeing the ground and working out exactly where he was. But as the fog cleared slightly, he got a terrible shock. He was in the center of New York, heading directly for a building! He managed to avoid it and several other skyscrapers, weaving in and out, wingtips almost scraping some walls.

Crash!

The end came at 9:49 AM when Smith smashed the bomber directly into the side of the Empire State Building. The plane hit the 78th and 79th floors, tearing a huge hole in the building and starting a fierce fire. Fourteen people died, including Lieutenant-Colonel Smith.

The Empire State Building, completed in 1931, is one of the most well-known and recognizable skyscrapers on the New York City skyline.

"The plane exploded within the building. There were five or six seconds—I was tottering on my feet trying to keep my balance—and three-quarters of the office was instantaneously consumed in a sheet of flame."

Catherine O'Connor, quoted in history1900s.about.com/od/1940s/a/empirecrash.htm

RESCUE!

Rescuers had little choice but to use the elevators of the Empire State Building to take badly injured victims to the ground. They did not know that part of the plane's engine had damaged the cables that held the elevators in their shafts. When one of the cables snapped, an elevator car fell straight down its shaft all the way from the 75th floor. Amazingly, Betty Lou Oliver, who was inside the elevator, survived the 1,000-feet (300 m) fall.

A view of the hole created by the B-25 bomber in the side of the Empire State Building. You can see part of the wreckage of the plane hanging from the 78th floor.

Collision Over the Grand Canyon, 1956

"Salt Lake, 718 ... ah ... we're going in!" These chilling words, heard faintly on a radio transmission, were the last from the crew of a United Airlines plane that crashed in 1956. They provided the only clue to the sudden disappearance of not one, but two, planes on the morning of June 30, over the remote region of the Grand Canyon in Arizona.

It was only later that day, when a small plane spotted burning wreckage below, that the terrible truth began to emerge. Both planes had plunged deep into the canyon. A military helicopter made a flight into the canyon the next morning, but it was clear that there were no survivors of this crash. The main work for rescue teams was to recover bodies, and to discover what had gone wrong.

AT-A-GLANCE

Date: June 30, 1956
Time: 10:32 AM
Flights: United Airlines Flight 718 and Trans World Airlines Flight 2
Place: Grand Canyon, Arizona
Crash: Midair collision
Deaths: 128—117 passengers and 11 crew

The planes collided over the remote and rugged region of the Grand Canyon.

Sifting through the wreckage

Helicopters took accident investigators into the canyon. Examining the wreckage was dangerous and difficult work. Parts of the United Airlines plane had fallen onto steep ledges high on the sides of the canyon. Eventually the investigators found pieces of wreckage from one plane marked with paint from the other. It was clear that the two planes had collided in midair.

Two rescue workers look at part of the wreckage of the Trans World Airlines plane lying on the floor of the canyon.

TWO YEARS ON

Both aircraft were flying in uncontrolled airspace—a part of the sky where there is no air traffic control service. It was up to the pilots to keep a lookout for other planes. Investigators concluded that the collision happened because of storm clouds blocking the pilots' view. Several other accidents around the same time raised public concern about the safety of flying. Within two years, new and improved systems of air traffic control were operating in the United States, which quickly reduced the number of accidents.

Munich, 1958

It was a happy Manchester United soccer team that boarded Flight BE609 on its way home from a European Cup playoff in Yugoslavia. The team was through to the next round. The plane had to land at Reim Airport in Munich, West Germany, for refueling. By the time it took off again, heavy snow was falling. Then came disaster!

BREAKING NEWS

February 6, 1958, Munich, West Germany ...

In blizzard conditions, an aircraft has crashed after skidding off the end of the runway. It appears to have hit a building and burst into flames. There are reports that the plane was carrying the entire Manchester United soccer team. It is not yet known if there are any injuries.

ELIZABETHAN CLASS
RMA LORD BURGHLEY

Rescue workers battle through snowy conditions to reach the wreckage of the *Lord Burghley* after the plane skidded and crashed off the end of the runway.

Death toll

Sadly, it quickly became clear to those who dashed to the wreckage that many people were badly injured, and many others were dead. The crash killed 23 of the 43 people on board the plane. Among the dead were eight Manchester United players, as well as club officials and journalists. Two other players who survived were so badly injured they never played soccer again.

How did it happen?

The first investigation into the crash blamed the pilot, Captain James Thain, for trying to take off without deicing the plane's wings. But a later investigation cleared the captain. It was found that the aircraft had hit slushy snow on the runway, which had slowed it down and prevented it from taking off.

Manchester United players Dennis Viollet (left) and Albert Scanton in their beds at Isar Hospital in Munich. Eight Manchester United players died in the crash.

Collision at Tenerife, 1977

In cloud and light rain, Pan Am Flight 1736 from the United States eased onto the runway at Los Rodeos Airport in Tenerife. The flight, full of passengers, had been due to land on the neighboring island of Las Palmas, but a terrorist bomb had closed that airport.

Many other planes were also diverted to Los Rodeos that day, including a Dutch KLM flight from Amsterdam. But by the time Las Palmas Airport reopened later in the afternoon, the light rain had turned into thick fog at Los Rodeos.

Explosion
On board the Pan Am flight and the KLM plane, crews and passengers were impatient to get away. Following instructions from the airport traffic controllers, both planes began to move toward the runway. Minutes later there was a massive explosion.

This computer image shows what happened as the two planes collided. The Pan Am plane (below) swerved, while the KLM plane (above) tried to take off.

The grim aftermath of the crash—burnt-out wreckage lies on the runway at Los Rodeos Airport in Tenerife.

Misunderstandings

The investigation that followed the crash revealed a series of misunderstandings between both plane crews and the air traffic controllers. The KLM pilot thought he had clearance (permission) to take off. Meanwhile the Pan Am pilot was warning air traffic control that his plane was still on the runway.

Suddenly the Pan Am pilot saw the KLM plane heading directly toward him through the thick fog. Desperately he swerved to the left. The KLM pilot tried to take off. But it was too late. The KLM plane struck the Pan Am plane, then dropped back to the runway, skidded and burst into flames.

Tenerife: The Aftermath

No one in the airport actually saw the crash—the fog was too dense. When people heard the explosion they thought at first that it was another terrorist attack. Thick, black smoke from the burning wreckage quickly covered the airport as emergency services struggled to reach the scene.

When they *did* arrive, firefighters thought the burning wreckage was all from one plane. Only after about 20 minutes did they realize there was a second burning plane farther down the runway.

Rescuing survivors

None of the people on board the KLM flight escaped the inferno that engulfed the plane. But brave firefighters and rescue workers plunged into the burning Pan Am plane to pull out survivors. Other passengers managed to scramble out onto the plane's left wing and jump to safety. It took until the following day to put out the fires completely.

EYEWITNESS

"Get off! Get off! Get off!"
Words of the co-pilot on Pan Am Flight 1736 as he sees the KLM plane approaching, desperately telling the pilot to steer off the runway.

One of the survivors of the crash is rushed to the hospital in Tenerife. With 583 fatalities, the crash remains the worst in aviation history.

After the crash

Around 70 experts from Spain, the Netherlands, the United States, and the two airline companies were involved in the crash investigation. The crash was the worst in the history of flying, and everyone wanted to make sure that the same mistakes could not happen again.

Thirty years after the crash, relatives of the victims came back to remember and mourn their loved ones at the crash memorial site in Mesa Mota, near Los Rodeos airport.

TEN YEARS ON

As a consequence of the crash, there were major changes to the way pilots and traffic controllers communicate. It was made a rule worldwide that air crews and air traffic controllers use standard English phrases to avoid any misunderstandings. Many airlines also installed equipment to allow crews to see better in fog.

Plunge into the Potomac, 1982

It was a bitterly cold day in Washington, DC, with heavy snowfalls. Many offices and businesses in the city closed early so that people could begin to make their way home. The snowy roads were jammed with traffic. At Washington National Airport, the authorities temporarily closed the airport so that snowplows could free the runway of snow.

Delayed

Like many other flights that day, Air Florida Flight 90 was delayed by the closing of the airport. When the plane did start its takeoff, at 3:59 PM, it reached a height of only 35 feet (107 m) before plunging back toward the ground.

Ice on the wings

It was later found that the plane was in the air for just 30 seconds before it crashed. The investigation that followed revealed that the crew had failed to deice the engines and wings of the plane properly.

BREAKING NEWS

January 13, 1982, Washington, DC ...
News is coming in that a plane has crashed into 14th Street Bridge over the Potomac River. Eyewitnesses on the bridge reported hearing the roar of engines, then seeing the plane smash into the traffic on the bridge before falling into the frozen river below. Washington is experiencing one of the worst snowstorms of the winter, and Washington National Airport was closed for a time this morning. Traffic in the city is gridlocked, and the emergency services are having problems responding to this situation.

SAVING LIVES

"That doesn't seem right, does it?" These words were spoken by the copilot of Air Florida Flight 90 just before its fateful 30-second flight. His words were ignored by the plane's pilot. Some of the main lessons learned from this crash were the importance of teamwork and clear communication in the cockpit of a plane. Pilots are not always right, and crew members need to have the confidence to point out problems and mistakes.

The 14th Street Bridge across the Potomac River is in fact several bridges, as seen here. The plane struck the middle bridge and plunged into the water between this and the right-hand bridges.

Potomac: Emergency Response

Horrified onlookers on 14th Street Bridge watched as the plane disappeared into the Potomac River. Only the tail of the plane remained visible above the ice, and clinging to the tail were six people who had managed to scramble out of the crashed aircraft.

Freezing

The situation was desperate. With the water temperature around freezing, every minute counted—no one can survive for long in such conditions. But the people on shore were helpless. The broken ice and freezing water made it impossible to swim out to help the survivors.

Part of the crashed plane is recovered from the icy waters of the Potomac River in January 1982.

EYEWITNESS

"More people arrived near the shore from the bridge but nobody could do anything. The ice was broken up and there was no way to walk out there. It was so eerie, an entire plane vanished except for a tail section, the survivors, and a few pieces of plane debris."

Eyewitness account on en.wikipedia.org/wiki/Air_Florida_Flight_90

Heroism

On the ground the emergency services were finding it difficult to get to the scene along icy roads and through gridlocked traffic. When help finally arrived, at 4:20 PM, it was from the air—a police helicopter. The helicopter crew lowered a line to the survivors and started to pull them one by one toward the shore. One of the passengers, later identified as Arland D. Williams Jr., twice passed the line on to other more badly injured survivors. By the time the helicopter returned to pull him to safety, he had disappeared beneath the icy waters.

RESCUE!

There were many examples of bravery and heroism in the Potomac River rescue. One of the survivors, Priscilla Tirado, was so frozen and weak she was unable to hold onto the line thrown down from the helicopter. As she slipped back into the icy waters, one bystander, Lenny Skutnik, stripped off his coat and boots and dived in. He saved Priscilla Tirado's life.

Rescue workers load a victim of the crash into a helicopter. You can see just how bad conditions were on the ground from this photo.

Day of Terror, 2001

Probably the most famous air crashes of all time took place in September 2001 in the United States. These crashes were not accidents but part of a deliberately planned terrorist attack, designed to cause death and destruction on a massive scale. Thousands of people lost their lives as a result.

Out of a clear blue sky

Tuesday September 11, was a beautiful day in New York City. Many people were making their way to their offices in the twin towers of the World Trade Center. At over 110 stories tall, these towers rose well above New York's other skyscrapers.

Then, at 8:46 AM, the unthinkable happened. A plane flew directly into the North Tower, between the 95th and 103rd floors. It exploded in a huge fireball, instantly killing everyone on the plane and many office workers. People on the floors above the explosion were unable to escape down the emergency stairs because of the fierce fires below.

Moment of impact: with the North Tower already burning, a second plane crashes into the South Tower of the World Trade Center, causing a massive explosion.

Seventeen minutes later, another plane appeared low over the city skyline. This one crashed into the South Tower, again causing a massive explosion.

Emergency response

Hundreds of firefighters and police officers began arriving at the World Trade Center. Some firefighters headed up the stairs in the towers, laden with all the equipment they would need to fight the fires far above them.

The aftermath of the crashes: firefighters walk through the rubble where the towers of the World Trade Center once stood.

SAVING LIVES

Most of the firefighters and police officers who went into the towers carried radios. Normally they used these radios to keep in contact with each other and with the control center. But the communication systems in the towers had been damaged in the crash. Many of the radios would not work. It made it impossible for rescuers inside the building to know what was going on outside.

EYEWITNESS

"…one of the most powerful things I will never forget is walking past firefighters who were walking up the stairs as I was walking down."

Brendan MacWade, survivor from the North Tower

Day of Terror: The Consequences

The towers of the World Trade Center were built to withstand a plane crash. However, the heat of the two fires was so intense that it quickly began to melt the steel frame that supported the buildings.

The towers collapse

The South Tower was the first to collapse, at 9:59 AM, crushing everyone inside as it fell. Immediately, all rescuers in the North Tower were ordered to get out as fast as possible. But because of the problems with the radios, many of the rescuers never heard the command. When the North Tower collapsed 29 minutes later, hundreds of firefighters and police officers lost their lives.

AT-A-GLANCE

Date: September 11, 2001 (often referred to as 9/11)

Time: 8:46 AM: 1st plane hits the North Tower of the World Trade Center
9:03 AM 2nd plane hits the South Tower
9:37 AM 3rd plane crashes into the Pentagon, Washington, DC
10:03 AM 4th plane crashes into a field in Pennsylvania

Flights: American Airlines Flight 11; United Airlines Flight 175; American Airlines Flight 77; United Airlines Flight 93

Cause of crashes: Terrorist attack

Deaths: 2,995, including 19 hijackers

A helicopter surveys the damage caused by the third hijacked plane, which crashed into the Pentagon in Washington, DC.

Who did it?

It soon became clear that the attacks were the work of an organization called al-Qaeda. The al-Qaeda terrorists hijacked four planes after they had taken off, then deliberately crashed them. The third plane was flown into the Pentagon, the headquarters of the US Department of Defense in Washington, DC, while the fourth crashed into a field in Pennsylvania. It seems that some of the passengers on this plane fought the hijackers, forcing the plane to miss its intended target.

On the eighth anniversary of the 9/11 attacks, people walk past the "Tribute in Lights," powerful laser beams that mark out in the sky exactly where the two towers once stood.

ONE YEAR ON

Al-Qaeda was based in Afghanistan. When the government of Afghanistan refused to hand over the leader of the organization, Osama bin Laden, a military coalition, led by the United States, attacked. One year later, many al-Qaeda members had been hunted down. But Osama bin Laden has never been caught.

The Flight 447 Mystery, 2009

On June 1, 2009, during its journey from Rio de Janeiro, Brazil, to Paris, France, Air France Flight 447 disappeared from the skies. Although search and rescue teams soon discovered what had happened, *why* it happened remains a mystery.

Debris in the sea

In the days and weeks after the crash, searchers found parts of the plane, and some bodies, in the sea. It was clear that the plane had fallen rapidly and crashed into the Atlantic Ocean. But to understand exactly what had gone wrong, investigators needed to find the plane's "black boxes."

The plane's tail, in Air France colors, is recovered from the Atlantic Ocean.

Searching information

Black boxes are, in fact, usually bright red to make them easier to spot. They contain recordings and data for every flight—information that can give investigators vital clues about what was happening in the minutes before a crash.

Black boxes are also equipped with "pingers" that send out signals once they hit water. Special listening devices can pick up the signals and help to locate the boxes. This needs to be done quickly though—the signals stop after about 30 days, when the batteries run down.

Searching the ocean

The French government sent naval ships and a nuclear submarine to look for the black boxes. They also sent ships equipped with mini-submarines. These mini-subs could dive thousands of feet below the ocean surface to where much of the wreckage of the plane now lies.

ONE YEAR ON

In the year after the crash there were three separate searches for the black boxes from Flight 447. Investigators were able to narrow their search to a few square miles. But the plane crashed over an area of ocean with a vast, undersea mountain range. The depth of the water, and the rugged landscape of the ocean floor, makes it difficult to know if anyone will ever recover the plane's black boxes.

The French mini-submarine *Nautile* was one of the submarines used to search for the plane's black boxes.

Learning from the Past

Every crash described in this book is a tragedy for those who were killed and injured, and their families. But it is important to remember that every day thousands of planes crisscross the skies above us without mishap. Travel by plane is extremely safe.

Safety improvements

One of the reasons that air travel is so safe is because people have learned important lessons from previous crashes. Many of the accidents described in this book led directly to improvements in safety. For example, the investigation after the Manchester disaster in 1985 (see page 7) resulted in many changes. They included new fire-retardant materials inside planes so that fire would not spread so quickly. The layout inside planes was also altered to allow people more time to escape in a fire.

A pilot and copilot at the controls of a large plane as it takes off.

Air traffic control

Other accidents have led to changes in the way aircraft are guided through the air and on runways. After the collision over the Grand Canyon (see pages 10–11), the US government set up the Federal Aviation Agency. The agency was put in charge of all air traffic control systems in the United States. The 1977 runway crash in Tenerife (see pages 14–17) resulted in all pilots being required to use standard English phrases when talking to air traffic control—no matter what part of the world they were operating in.

Chesley Sullenberger, pilot of US Airways Flight 1549, who successfully ditched the plane in the Hudson River after losing power in both engines. Sullenberger was the last to evacuate the aircraft after checking the passenger cabin twice to ensure that no one remained on board.

SAVING LIVES

Sometimes when disaster strikes, it is quick-thinking pilots who act to save lives. On January 15, 2009, a passenger flight from New York City hit a flock of birds just after takeoff. Both of the plane's engines immediately shut down. Unable to reach a runway, the pilot turned his plane toward the Hudson River and glided down onto the water. Thanks to the bravery and skill of the pilot, Chesley "Sully" Sullenberger, and his crew, all 155 passengers were rescued unharmed.

Glossary

air traffic control The ground-based staff who direct the movement of aircraft. The main purpose of air traffic control is to ensure that planes are kept apart so that they do not collide with each other, as well as providing information to pilots.

al-Qaeda A terrorist organization that has cells in many countries. It was responsible for the 9/11 attacks on the United States.

black box A machine, also known as a flight recorder, that records data for every flight, as well as the words spoken by the crew in the cockpit. The machine is in fact usually painted bright red.

canyon A deep valley with cliffs on either side.

clearance Official authority or permission.

communication system A device that allows people to talk to each other.

copilot The second pilot on a plane, also known as first officer. The copilot would take over if anything happened to the pilot.

deice Remove ice.

divert Turn from one direction or place to another.

emergency services The police, fire, and ambulance services.

fireball A ball of flame or fire.

fire-retardant A substance that helps to stop or slow the spread of fire.

gridlock A traffic jam affecting a whole network of intersecting streets, making it impossible for cars to move in any direction.

hijack Take over control of a plane, or other vehicle, illegally.

mini-submarine A small submarine.

nuclear submarine A submarine powered by nuclear fuel.

pilot The person who flies and is in charge of a plane.

radio transmission A communication sent by a radio to a receiver.

skyscraper A very tall building.

slushy Describes snow that is melting and wet.

terrorist attack An attack intended to bring terror and harm to innocent people in order to achieve a political aim.

uncontrolled airspace An area in the sky where there is no air traffic control service.

wreckage The remains of something that has been damaged or destroyed.

Further Information

Books

Air Disasters by Michael Woods and Mary B. Woods (Lerner, 2007)
Disasters: Anatomy of a Plane Crash by Amie Jane Leavitt (Velocity, 2010)
Flight: 100 Years of Aviation by R. G. Grant (Dorling Kindersley, 2010)
September 11: A Primary Source History by Alan Wachtel (Gareth Stevens, 2009)
Terrorism Alert! by Lynn Peppas and Sydney Newton (Crabtree Publishing, 2006)

Web Sites

www.aerospaceweb.org/question/history/q0311.shtml
Information about and pictures of the Empire State Building crash.

www.airsafe.com/airline.htm
Up-to-date information about air safety and crashes worldwide.

http://aviation-safety.net/index.php
Information about plane crashes, investigations, and safety measures.

www.faa.gov
Home page of the Federal Aviation Administration.

Index